D1788495

597.53 SCH	Schlein, Miriam.	1364
	The dangerous life of the sea horse.	
		$11.66
DATE DUE	BORROWER'S NAME	ROOM NO.
11/10	Clint	Webb
	Clint	

597.53 SCH Schlein, Miriam. 1364

The dangerous life of the sea horse.

**ALTERNATE LEARNING CENTER
LUCAS COUNTY OFFICE EDUCATION**

674004 53858A 03990E

The Dangerous Life
of the Sea Horse

Books by MIRIAM SCHLEIN

Project Panda Watch

What the Elephant Was

The Dangerous Life of the Sea Horse

The Dangerous Life of the Sea Horse

by MIRIAM SCHLEIN

illustrated by GWEN COLE

ATHENEUM ○ 1986 ○ NEW YORK

Acknowledgments

The author expresses her thanks to Dr. C. L. Smith, Department of Ichthyology, American Museum of Natural History, for his counsel. The illustrator would also like to thank Dr. Smith, Dr. James Atz and the Miami Seaquarium.

Library of Congress Cataloging-in-Publication Data

Schlein, Miriam.
    The dangerous life of the sea horse.

    Includes index.
    Summary: Follows the life cycle of the sea horse, a fish with a prehensile tail and body armor, describing its physical characteristics, habits, and natural environment.
    1. Sea horses—Juvenile literature.   [1. Sea horses]   I. Cole, Gwen, ill.   II. Title.
QL638.S9S35   1986   597.53   85-26857
ISBN 0-689-31180-X

Text copyright © 1986 by Miriam Schlein
Illustrations copyright © 1986 by Gwen Cole
All rights reserved
Published simultaneously in Canada by Collier Macmillan Canada
Printed and bound by Maple-Vail, Binghamton, New York
Designed by Marilyn Marcus
First edition

CONTENTS

1 Danger All Around 7

2 A Drifting Home 14

3 The Big Wave 19

4 New Neighbors 20

5 What the Sea Horses Saw 25

6 A Strange Visitor 28

Different Kinds of Sea Horses 30

Index 32

The Dangerous Life
of the Sea Horse

Walking along the shore one day, you may find one. You nearly missed it; it is twisted and hidden in a large glob of seaweed. But there it is.

A sea horse.

Its scientific name is *hippocampus*. In Greek this means horse-caterpillar—a strange name. But if you look at it, its tiny head does look something like the head of a horse? And its body is long, like that of a caterpillar.

The sea horse you found is dead. Like all fish—and it *is* a fish—it cannot live outside of the water; and this one was thrown up on the shore, perhaps in a storm.

Pick it up. It feels hard and bony. That's because a sea horse has a skeleton *outside* its body as well as inside. The outer skeleton is made up of many rings of bone with prickly sharp points on them.

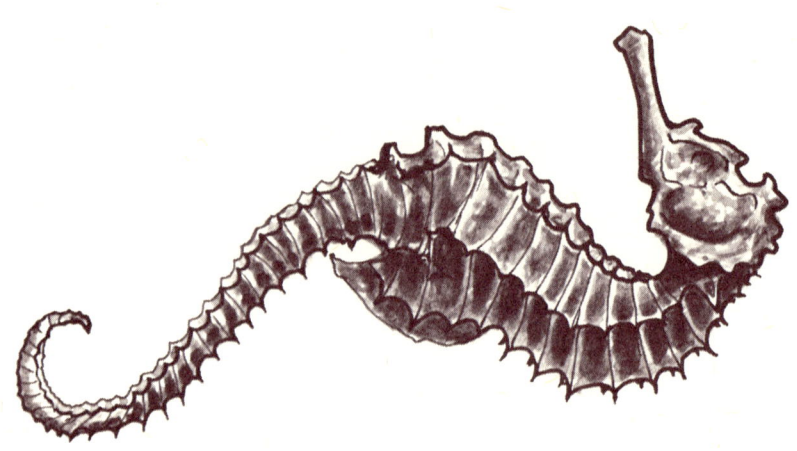

It doesn't look like any other kind of fish, does it? What kind of life did this strange little creature have?

The outer skeleton is covered with a thin layer of skin.

The inner skeleton has a backbone and provides support.

Danger All Around 1

The sea horse glided down through the water. He was headed for some seaweed that grew like a fat bush on the ocean bottom.

A huge silvery shark approached. Sharks sometimes eat sea horses. But the sea horse was in luck. The shark must not have been hungry, for it just slid by, ignoring him.

Reaching the seaweed bush, the sea horse grabbed on by his tail to a branch. Then his body began to twitch and wiggle.

Was it from fear?

No. Something else was happening. He bent his head several times as though bowing. Then, from a small opening in his underbelly, a batch of tiny sea horses burst out from inside him and spread out in the water around him.

The sea horse was giving birth.

Baby sea horses are born in an unusual way. It is the *father* that gives birth to the babies, not the mother.

About six weeks ago, he and a female sea horse had mated, clinging to each other, belly to belly. Through a long, thin tube (called an *ovipositor*) the female had placed eggs in a pouch on the male's underbelly. Here, in the pouch, lying in the softness, the eggs developed and finally hatched.

Now, ready to be born, the young pop out in batches. Each one is tiny; about one-fourth of an inch long (about 6 mm). They are perfectly formed—tiny miniatures of their mother and father.

For two days, the father has been giving birth. This is the sixth batch that has left his pouch. Now, weak and tired, he clings to the seaweed, as his last batch of little ones spread about in the water around him.

There are twenty of them. As soon as they leave the pouch and enter the ocean, they are on their own.

For a few seconds, they drift around every which way. Then, heads up, they ride up to the ocean surface.

A sea horse goes up and down in the water with the help of its *swim bladder.* As it swims upward, gas expands in the swim bladder. This gas comes from the bloodstream. To stop moving upward, the sea horse has to let some of this gas out, back into the bloodstream. To go back down, even more gas must be let out. So, a sea horse goes up and down by changing the amount of gas in its swim bladder.

When they are small, like this, they are food for all kinds of fish, large and small. Can these tiny creatures survive on their own in the ocean, with so many dangers around them?

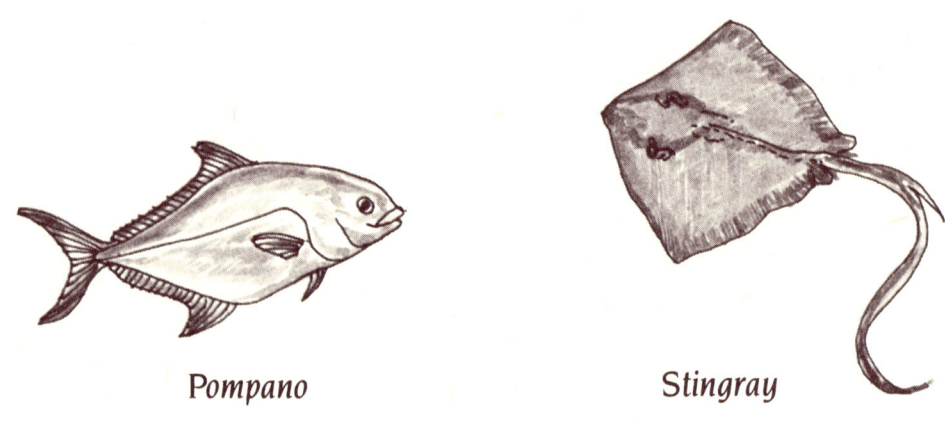

Pompano

Stingray

Moray Eel

Barracuda

Albacore

Dogfish Shark

Spadefish

Grunt

Snook

2 A Drifting Home

The open water is not a safe place for sea horses. But close by, a large piece of seaweed drifts in the current. The tiny sea horses swim toward it. They will be safer, hidden in the seaweed.

Many fish swim quite fast by propelling themselves with a back-and-forth swishing movement of the tail. But a sea horse, with its upright posture, is not built for speed. It swims very slowly.

By flicking the delicate fan-shaped fin on its back very fast—thirty-five beats per second (more than two thousand times a minute)—it swims forward.

To go left or right, it steers with its small side fins. It also uses its head to establish direction, facing left to go left; right to go right.

Heading toward the seaweed, flicking their fins, the little sea horses swim for the first time. Then, curling their little tails back, they each grip a hair-sized branch and hang on.

Like a monkey, the sea horse has a tail that can be used to grasp things. This is called a *prehensile* (pree-*hen*-sul) tail.

Now the sea horses are ready for their first meal.

Drifting through the ocean are masses of tiny sea life, many so small you can see them only with a microscope. Some are little shrimplike forms, others are like little worms. Some are larva of fish or sponges or crabs. This mass of tiny life is called *plankton*. It is what sea horses eat.

They suck in hundreds of bits of plankton, very fast, through their tubelike snouts. Then they rest.

Sea horses sleep for very short periods. They have no eyelids, and never close their eyes, so scientists aren't sure exactly how long a sea horse sleeps. But they do know it's just a short time.

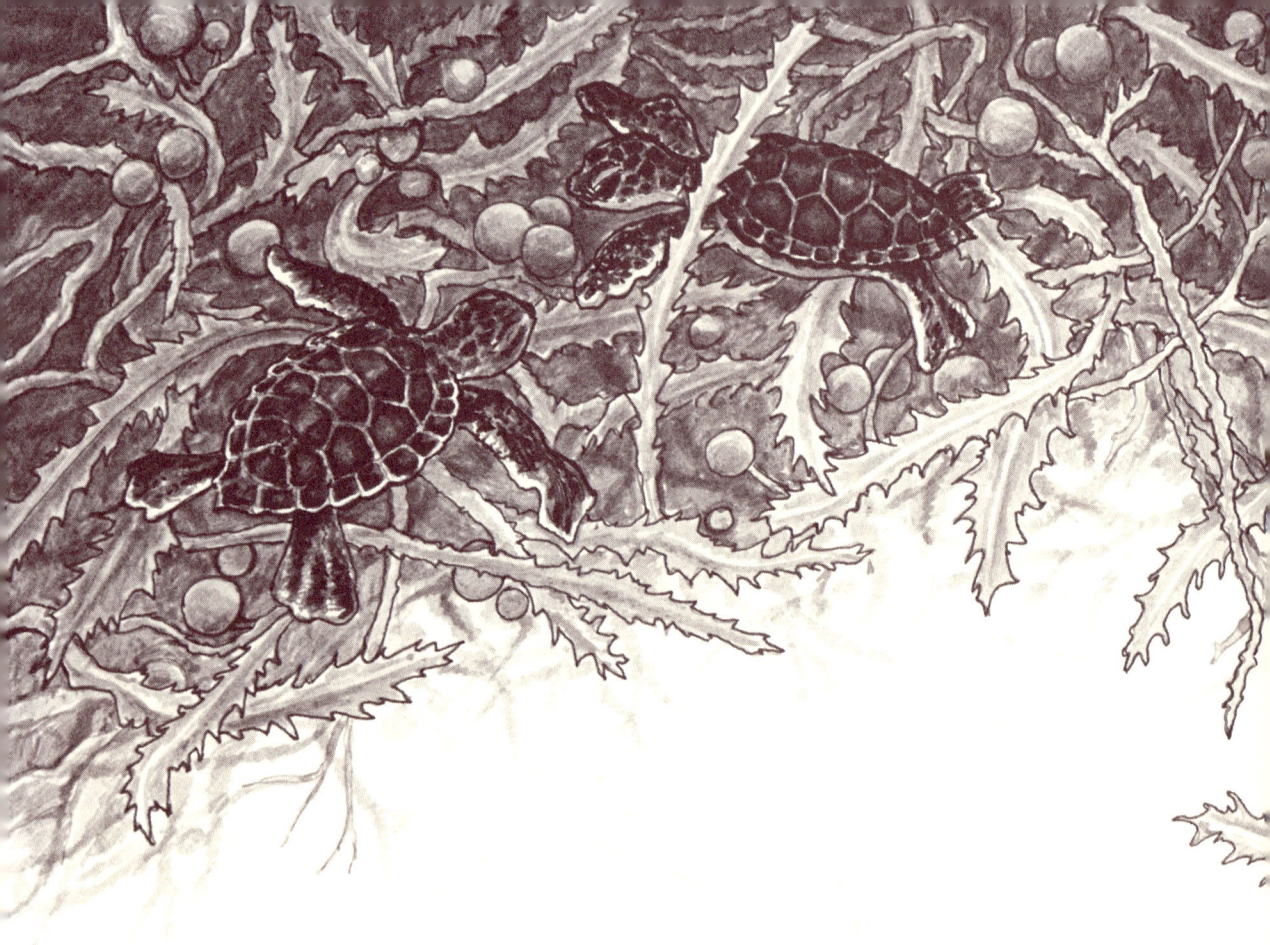

The sea horses are not alone in this green tangle of seaweed. The seaweed, as it drifts in the ocean, is home to other creatures as well. There are baby sea turtles. There are other sea horses, too.

Sea turtles eat sea horses. Grown sea horses also sometimes eat baby sea horses. But luckily for the little sea horses, they are all living in different parts of the seaweed.

The Big Wave 3

For four months the sea horses live in the drifting clump of seaweed. They've grown a lot in this time. They are now about three inches long (8 cm). Then something happens that changes their lives.

A storm comes up, bigger than most. The water churns. The strand of seaweed bounces up and down. After one tremendous wave, with the water pushing this way and that, the sea horses lose their grip and are swept off.

Three of them, clinging to each other by their tails, are pulled downward in the wild water.

They bump into a school of small fish who are hovering below, waiting out the storm. Some of the fish turn toward the sea horses, then turn away.

When the sea horses were smaller, these three-inch fish would have eaten them. But not now. They're too big. Also, their outer skeleton—those bony rings around their body—is harder. It's like a suit of armor. The rings have prickly points on them as well. Many fish now leave them alone.

4 New Neighbors

When the storm dies down, the sea horses have been carried by the waves and currents to a new place. It's like an underwater garden. Purple and pink and green forms grow out of the ocean bottom. Some are round. Some have long thin arms. Others are bushy.

It's a coral reef.
The sea horses twist their tails around the coral. Again, they've been lucky. Again, they have found a good home.

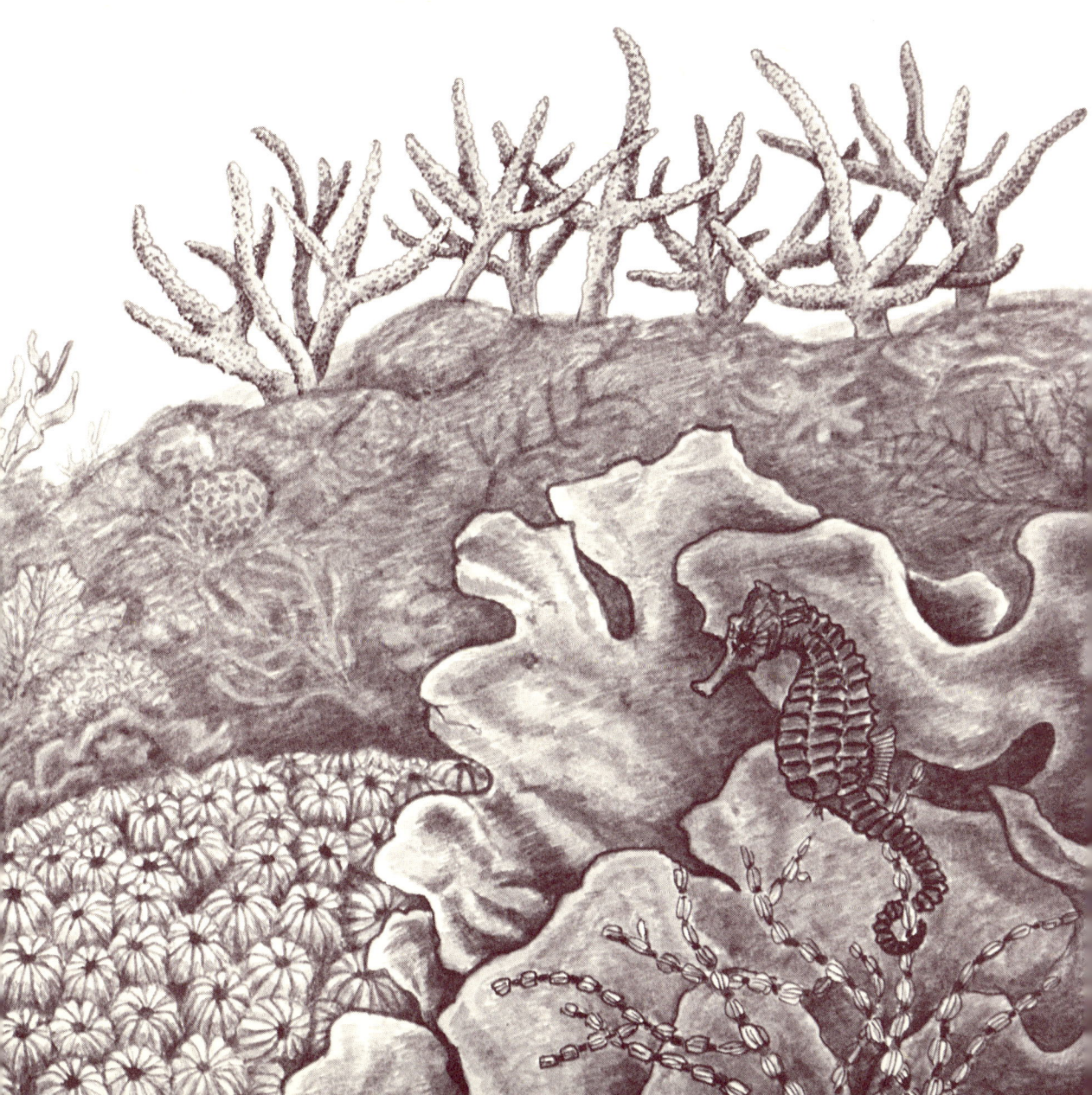

Many creatures live in the coral reef. There are starfish and shellfish and many other fish of different shapes and colors. Moray eels live hidden in the coral, sliding out at night to hunt.

There are sea anemones (uh-*nem*-oh-neez) that look like big flowers on the ocean bottom. But they're not flowers; they're animals that hunt for prey. And those are not leaves, waving gently in the water. They are tentacles. They let out poison threads that paralyze a fish, then pull it in, to be eaten by the anemone mouth in the center.

Larger fish cruise the reef; tuna and sharks. A barracuda swims by, its big mouth open, its sharp teeth showing.

Small fish swim off and hide in the coral. The sea horses can't swim fast. But they have a different way of hiding.

They hide right where they are by changing color and blending in with their surroundings so it's hard to see them.

When they lived in the seaweed, they were grayish green, like the seaweed. Now they have turned a deep pink—coral color—to match the coral they are near. Hiding by blending in this way is called *camouflage* (*cam-uh-flazh*).

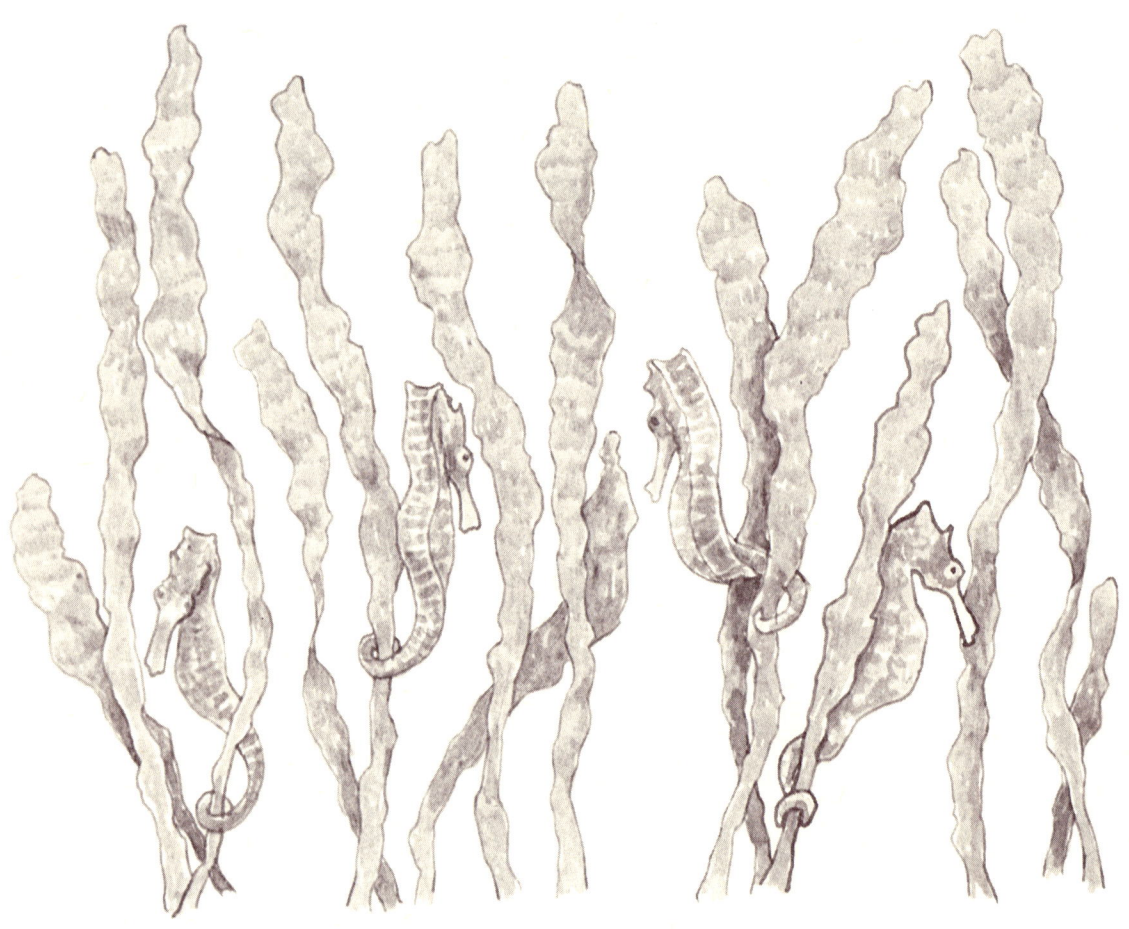

What the Sea Horses Saw 5

The coral reef is made of small creatures called polyps (*pah*-lips). At one end of a polyp's body is a mouth. It lets out a substance that forms a hard cup around the other end of its body. The polyp can pull itself into this hard cup in times of danger.

The coral reef is made of many thousands of these hard cups, one on top of the other, from polyps that have died and from those still living.

And so, from the bodies of these small sea creatures, a place of beauty is made.

From time to time the sea horses drifted and swam from one coral strand to another, changing color according to the color of the particular coral close to them.

Moving about, they were always on the lookout for danger. Sea horses have unusual eyes, to help them do this. Each eye works independently. Thus, a sea horse can be looking straight ahead with one eye and down at the sea bottom with the other.

There was a lot going on in the coral reef. Other sea creatures were eating and being eaten. A moray eel crept out to catch its prey. A green parrotfish nibbled at the coral with its sharp teeth, eating the polyps inside.

There were little wrasse fish clinging to the parrotfish's mouth, eating, in turn, the mashed-up leftover bits.

All these things could be seen in the coral reef.

6 A Strange Visitor

One day, a new kind of creature appeared; a stranger to the sea. It was not brightly colored like the others, but black, with bubbles coming out.

A black arm reached out toward the sea horses. But that moment, a sharp-toothed barracuda drifted into sight.

The black creature moved off slowly, forgetting about the sea horses. The barracuda, which sometimes eats sea horses, this time had saved them.

A year went by. The sea horses were now six inches long (15 cm). They were full grown. They mated with other sea horses, clinging to each other, tails entwined. Six weeks later, their bodies twitching, the males gave birth to several hundred baby sea horses.

Some sea horses can live two or three years. They mate and have young many times.

Most baby sea horses do not survive the dangers of the sea. But many do, helped by the protections that nature has given them.

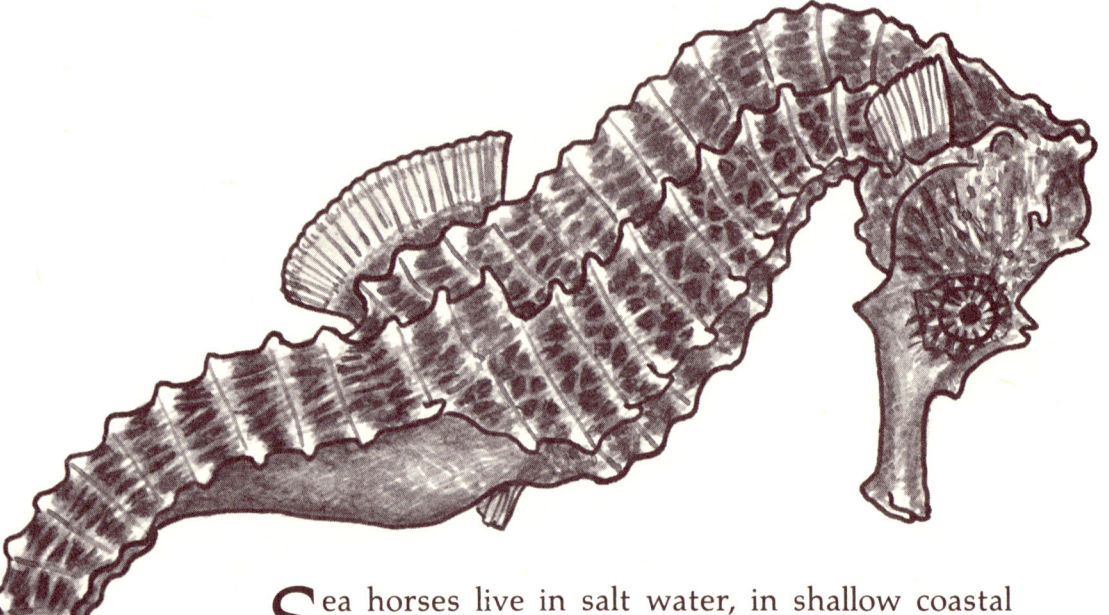

Pacific

Sea horses live in salt water, in shallow coastal areas, usually—but not always—in warm seas. There are about twenty-four different species (types) around the world.

The Pacific sea horse is the biggest—about one foot long (30 cm). It lives in the Pacific Ocean along the southern California coast, and as far south as Peru, South America. The scientific name of this species is *Hippocampus ingens*.

The dwarf sea horse is the smallest—one and one-half inches or less (about 4 cm). It lives in the Atlantic Ocean along the Florida coast and in the Gulf of Mexico. Dwarf sea horses live a shorter life (one year or less) than other types. The scientific name of this species is *Hippocampus zosterae*.

Dwarf

Different Kinds of Sea Horses

Lined

The sea horses in this book are known as lined sea horses. They are also sometimes called spotted sea horses. Their scientific name is *Hippocampus erectus*. They live in the Atlantic Ocean off the Florida coast, in the Caribbean Sea and the Gulf of Mexico. This is one of the few kinds of sea horse that is also found in cooler waters. They may also live along the Atlantic coast at times, as far north as Cape Cod, and even Nova Scotia.

Lined sea horses even have been found up to ten miles up the Hudson River, near New York City, where the water is still a bit salty from the sea. Normally, sea horses cannot live in polluted waters, so very few are now found in the Hudson River. The ones found there recently were greenish-brown.

Elsewhere, in warmer seas, sea horses are many beautiful colors—all shades of orange, red, yellow, as well as pearly white, gray, brown, tan, jet black and bright green.

Index

A

Anemone (sea), 22

B

Backbone, 5
Barracuda, 23, 28
Birth, 8, 9, 10
Body, 4, 5

C

Camouflage, 24
Color, 24, 31
Coral reef, 20, 21, 24, 25

D

Dwarf sea horse, 30

E

Eating, 15
Eel, 22
Egg pouch, 10, 11
Enemies, 7, 12, 13, 16, 22, 23
Eyes, 15, 26

F

Fins, 14
Food, 15

H

Habitat, 30, 31

L

Life span, 28
Lined sea horse, 31
Locomotion, 10, 14

M

Moray eel, 22, 27
Mouth, 15

O

Ovipositor, 9

P

Pacific sea horse, 30
Parrotfish, 27
Plankton, 15
Pollution, 31
Polyps, 25, 17
Pouch, 9

S

Scientific names, 3, 30, 31
Sea anemone, 22
Seaweed, 7, 14, 16
Shark, 7
Size, 9, 19, 28, 30
Skeleton, 4, 19
Sleep, 15
Species, 30, 31
Spotted sea horse, 31
Swim bladder, 10, 11

T

Tail, 7, 14
Turtles, 16

W

Wrasse fish, 27